IMAGES OF ENGLAND

NEWCASTLE WEST END

IMAGES OF ENGLAND

NEWCASTLE WEST END

RAY MARSHALL AND THE
NEWCASTLE EVENING CHRONICLE

TEMPUS

Frontispiece: Forth Lane, 1933. This was an old-world corner of Newcastle, which at this time was under threat of a rebuilding scheme. The entrance to the lane is still there on Westgate Road although there have been a few other changes. This picture first appeared in the *Evening Chronicle* and was used again on 25 October 1945, stating that Newcastle's early morning workers will be able to walk through lighted streets after 5 a.m. in future.

First published 2004

Tempus Publishing Limited
The Mill, Brimscombe Port,
Stroud, Gloucestershire, GL5 2QG
www.tempus-publishing.com

© Ray Marshall and the Newcastle Evening Chronicle, 2004

The right of Ray Marshall and the Newcastle Evening Chronicle to be identified as the Author of this work has been asserted in accordance with the Copyrights, Designs and Patents Act 1988.

British Library Cataloguing in Publication Data.
A catalogue record for this book is available from the British Library.

ISBN 0 7524 3351 2

Typesetting and origination by Tempus Publishing Limited.
Printed in Great Britain.

Contents

Westgate Road, *c.* 1948. Looking from the Literary and Philosophical Society library building (the Lit & Phil) the old *Evening Chronicle* building (Kemsley House) can be seen, and the Union Rooms. A laden horse and cart passes Barclays Bank and Pudding Chare as the driver delivers his wares. The main building on the opposite corner is the Norwich Union.

Introduction

This book is a tribute to those people who created the West End of Newcastle; the people of Scotswood, Elswick, Benwell and Fenham. When I chose this area as the subject of the book, I had envisaged all that might be left of that great sprawl of what was once row upon row of back-to-back houses and families living in overcrowded squalid conditions would be a small enclave, rough and uncompromising. But I soon found that these preconceived ideas were completely wrong. The West End has undergone yet more change and travelling through this area of town it is hard to connect the old and new.

But there is one thing that has remained constant throughout and that is the cheerfulness and friendliness of the people. A new colourful society has sprung up to replace the old one and the West End of Newcastle is thriving once again.

This book will take you on a journey most of which is within living memory. Our starting point will be on Westgate Road, close to St John's church, then moving outward in a westerly direction and passing the Old Assembly Rooms, which have seen many a brilliant and important event in the social life of the city since 1776.

Our journey up Westgate Road will take us up past the General Hospital and on to Denton Burn and eventually to Westerhope, where even today you can find sections of a Roman wall set amongst the modern housing estates that have sprung up in recent years. Although these ancient, small fragments don't look much today they are the remains of what was once, nearly 2,000 years ago, a wall of imposing dimensions, some 20ft high and patrolled by armed guards.

We will move west from the cattle market and past what was once the site of Marlborough Crescent bus station and onto Scotswood Road, the inspiration of the Geordie anthem, The Blaydon Races. Keeping close to the river, where today you can see business parks and vast green open spaces, we will look back at land where industrial giants who shaped the world once strode including the Elswick ordnance, engineering and locomotive works of Vickers Armstrong, once known as Armstrong, Whitworth & Co.

This book takes you through the streets that this industry spawned and the pubs where the workers drank.

In days gone by the mention of Newcastle's West End always brought to mind a dark, dour place, an area that spawned the type of community needed to create wealth for the nation, while living in abject poverty. That wealth was created in large industrial factories that lined the banks of the Tyne, turning out armaments, ships, trains and even leather, along with anything else the new industrialised world cried out for. But that convenient description hid a colourful society of diverse communities. The setting up of Lord Armstrong's works in the Elswick area of Newcastle in the late 1800s led in turn to the introduction of migrant workers from Ireland and Scotland and the creation of a massive multicultural society.

Over the years outward expansion has embraced the villages of Benwell, Fenham, Denton and Westerhope and included areas such as Scotswood to create the West End of Newcastle.

It was the coal hidden underground in these areas and the close proximity to the sea that meant this area became so important to the development and the prosperity of the North East. Unfortunately it did not follow that all local people would ultimately share in the spoils of business profit.

A map of Newcastle dated 1788 shows that the now thriving city was once not much more that a large village. There was Northumberland Street, Pilgrim Street, Percy Street, the Bigg Market and even Westgate Street. But outside that area, west of where the central station now stands, it was only farmland. Leaving the old Tyne Bridge you would have travelled less than a mile westward before you hit open countryside. In less that 200 years those vast expanses of ploughed fields went through a vast change as Newcastle became a city at the heart of Britain's industrial revolution.

Tyneside's economy was originally founded on the coal trade, mined on the banks of the Tyne long before the industrial revolution and shipped to the London markets. It is not surprising that the area become a major centre for coal-using industries. By the 1820s 2 million tons of coal a year was being shipped from the Tyne and this led to Newcastle's commercial development and the rapid expansion of the Northumberland and Durham coalfields in its wake.

Deeper pits were sunk and wagon ways were replaced by railways, followed by the development of manufacturing industries. Shipbuilding was originally established to help the coal trade became prosperous and then it diversified. Armaments and engineering industries with links to naval shipbuilding started to develop. William Armstrong's revolutionary gun was invented and by the end of the nineteenth century his works at Elswick and Scotswood employed over 25,000 workers. As Armstrong's industrial empire grew, so there followed an influx of migrant workers, English, Irish and Scottish, from all parts of the British Isles. A rapid expansion of housing followed, which in turn brought shops, pubs, churches and a massive new community on the western approaches to Newcastle.

Tyneside's over-dependence on a narrow range of industries, shipbuilding, armaments and the coal trade, was eventually to prove a liability. This book gives more than echoes from the past, it also shows how, despite the problems of its past, the West End of Newcastle is here to stay!

Ray Marshall, 2004

one

Westgate Road

Charleton's *History of Newcastle upon Tyne* tells us that a postern gate was built in the West Gate for the brethren of the Virgin Mary Hospital, that they had convenient access to their grounds outside the wall. It was from this postern that a famous sortie was made in the reign of Edward III against the army of King David of Scotland, camped outside in the Forth, waiting for a chance to attack the town. The passage states 'one night there marched forth a certain number of gallant gentlemen. They numbered at most 300 spears, a mere handful against the Scottish host, but bursting suddenly upon the camp of the sleeping enemy they succeeded in throwing them into confusion and capturing the Earl of Moray in his bed. They carried him with them into the town clad only in his night-dress.' The furious Scots assaulted the walls of the town, but were forced to draw back. The postern had gates of oak, iron doors and a heavy portcullis and was said to be very strong. Westgate Road is the oldest named street in Newcastle and is known as the great thoroughfare between the western entrance to the town, the citadel - the Castle Keep. Named after the West Gate on the City walls it has been one of the City's most important roads and has played a vital part in Newcastle's development. It runs along the course of a defensive ditch built just north of Hadrian's Wall and during the conversion of a local building into the Newcastle Arts Centre, in 1985, part of a mile castle on Hadrian's Wall was discovered. During the eighteenth century Westgate Road was almost totally composed of the residences of the 'important and well to do'. It was in the 1840s that the character of the area began to change. Although it remained predominantly private residences until around 1870, the occupants were becoming more often than not tradesmen. As the road branched out, the boundaries of Newcastle moved with it.

Bath Lane, 1948. Many of the buildings on Bath Lane were destined to be demolished bringing the 600 years old hidden walls of Newcastle's old town back into view. The widening of the road was also supposed to solve traffic problems in the area and show a 300ft stretch of city wall.

Bath Lane, 1958. Demolition was well underway and the Bath Lane site just about cleared. The round Durham Tower has now come back into view after being hidden for hundreds of years.

Bath Lane, 1954. The city council was recommended to acquire several properties from the junction of Bath Lane and Westgate Road, up to and including the Bath Hotel, and eventually an area with a depth of about 50ft was to be cleared.

Bath Lane, 1959. Where Bath Lane joins Westgate Road. Although there is a no entry sign a van can be seen facing up the road. Showing the onward and unstoppable march of traffic, the area in front of the city walls has become a car park. The bottom part of the Lane is now fully pedestrianised.

Bath Lane, 1961. The cars have now been vanquished from the Bath Lane site and the city wall has been framed with lawns and trees. The wall has been cleaned up, rose beds laid and seats sited to make the area a city centre oasis. Eventually the wall section and park will join up with the Stowell Street towers and wall, which was to be exposed to view on both sides.

Above: Westgate Road, *c.* 1933. Part of the tower of Westgate Road police station is tottering and ready to crash down. The station was being pulled down during extensive demolition work in this area.

Right: West End, *c.* 1910. A horse pulling a Newcastle Corporation refuse cart enjoys a brief rest in the sunshine, before continuing its journey through West Newcastle.

Overleaf: Bath Lane, 1962. As these sunbathers show, it is possible to leave the heavy traffic laden streets behind and relax, with just a flavour of history, on a hot day.

Westgate Road, 1850s. A superb drawing of old Westgate Road, looking back towards Newcastle. The road is lined with fine houses, walled and gardened. Prominent in the background is St Nicholas's Cathedral and the castle keep.

Spring Gardens, 1954. Children play in front of the Greyhound pub. This is the street where William Shield, born in Swalwell in 1748, made his musical debut. The brilliant musician went on to become Master of the King's Music and he wrote twenty operas, many of them performed at Covent Garden. William Shield was so highly thought of that when he died he was interred in Westminster Abbey. The Spring Gardens were once known as a place of genteel resort where the 'gay and fashionable were entertained in tents and amused with much singing', according to an old newspaper article. These concerts began around the year 1763.

The Poor Law Infirmary, *c.* 1919. The Infirmary on Westgate Road became the Wingrove Hospital in around 1920 and Newcastle General Hospital in around 1930.

Westgate Road, 1956. Traffic may be light outside the General Hospital, but the ambulance on the left of the picture still seems to be having trouble getting onto the roadway.

Westgate Road, 1964. The bus stop situated outside the General Hospital on Westgate Road was proving a menace. It caused hold-ups to ambulances leaving the hospital and fire engines leaving the nearby station. It also blocked the view of the main road for motorists entering from Brighton Grove and hampered their view of the zebra crossing.

Opposite above: General Hospital, 1970. Dolly patients help in the training of nurses at Newcastle General Hospital. Records of the hospital show that in 1891 there were 245 in-patients, 111 of them more or less bed-ridden and only one chief nurse and four assistants to care for them. This meant that each nurse on duty had more than sixty patients in her care. By 1930 the hospital had been enlarged from the original 225 beds to one of 540 beds and 123 staff.

Opposite below: Denton Bank, 1938. This picture shows the vast difference from the West Road of 1938 and the West Road of today in the Denton Burn area. A gentleman stands on the roadside in his plus fours waiting for an eastbound trolleybus with a Morris saloon standing by the kerbside. The lack of traffic and pedestrians makes for a strange scene when compared to the noisy, non-stop A69 trunk road of today. The trolley bus route had just been extended from the Denton Hotel to Denton Square that spring.

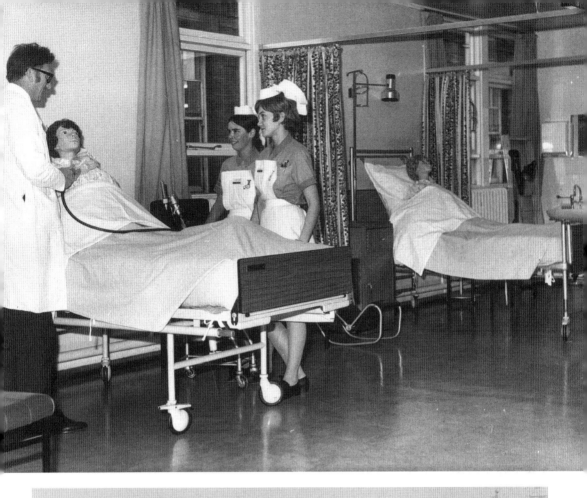

Denton Road, 1957. Trolley buses stand at the terminus of the weed–grown unmade path at the corner of Whickham View and Denton Road.

Denton Grove, 1970. This quaint row of colliery houses in an isolated street in Westerhope had been subjected to a wave of vandalism. Several of the homes become vacant and windows were being regularly broken and lead piping and gas water fittings stolen. The council was determined to combat this and moved in new tenants at the earliest opportunity.

Two Ball Lonnen, February, 1939. Europe was under the clouds of war and in Two Ball Lonnen, a group of excited children witness the first delivery of a consignment of ARP shelters.

Above: West Road, *c.* 1900. This old pub could be the original Fox and Hounds Inn, West Turnpike, on the West Road, of Newcastle.

Overleaf: West Newcastle, 1971. A poignant picture of two youngsters in the slums of West Newcastle. The moving picture became part of a housing campaign to highlight the problems of the time.

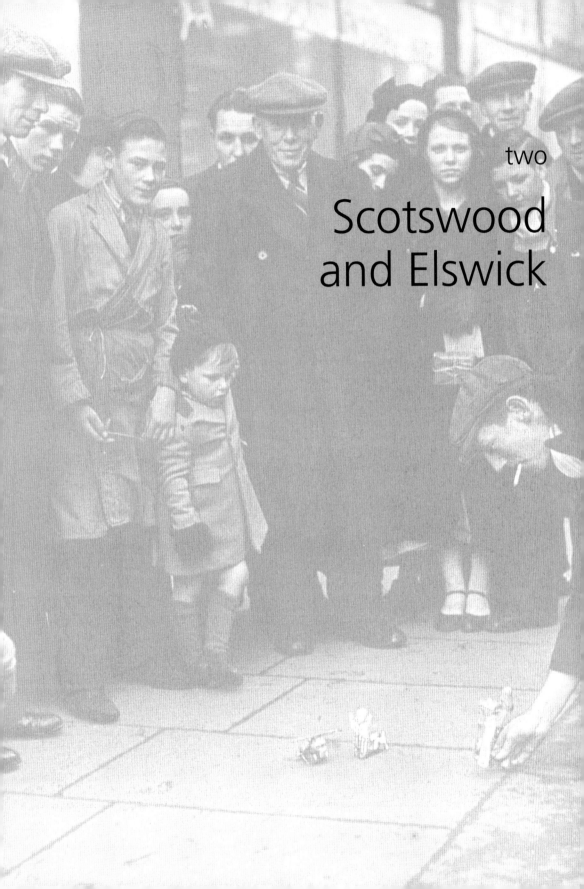

two

Scotswood
and Elswick

It could have been described as the Great Clearances as street after street of back-to-back housing was demolished to make way for a cleaner, more modern style of home for families that had struggled in the depths of poverty for years. Scotswood Road today is a greener and more pleasant place than it was in the days when Lord Armstrong's works dominated the area. Lord Armstrong brought jobs to people who needed to feed families, but the prosperity produced by his armaments factory didn't filter down to the workers. There were more pawn shops than in any other similar sized area in Britain. But it was the sheer scale of the slum clearance which impressed outside authorities, especially when those who were moved had to be found adequate housing while they waited for their chance to return to Scotswood. The legendary road, which has a special place in Geordie folklore, is now recovering and hopefully will soon take its rightful place as one of Tyneside's main thoroughfares.

Did the Elswick pitmen who betrayed Newcastle to the invading Scottish army over 350 years ago ever live it down? The pitmen were employed by John Osbourne, who was said to be a 'false rebellious Scot', to undermine the town walls. They did this so successfully that the 30,000 Scots managed to end the siege after five weeks of bitter fighting. 'The townsfolk,' wrote a contemporary, 'were but in all 1,500 men, wearied with continual watch and duty, though men of great courage, they fought gallantly to the last.' But maybe the pitmen were forgiven for it wasn't until 1835 that Elswick became officially part of Newcastle. The Scots, whose headquarters under General Leven during this phase of the Civil War, were at Elswick, 'a village about a mile to the west of Newcastle,' patrolled the Tyne from the island called the King's Meadows, long since dredged away.

Elswick was a flourishing mining community in the days around 1536 when coal was half the price on Tyneside as it was in London, and when you could buy a 'chaldron' of coal for half-a-crown. The old village was taken down in around 1810 to make way for the building of Elswick Hall, which became part of Elswick Park. A cemetery now stands where once pleasant country lanes led through renowned bramble hedgerows.

The Blaydon Races

I went to Blaydon Races
'Twas on the 9th of June
Eighteen Hundred and Sixty Two
On a summer's Afternoon
We took the bus from Balmbras
And she was heavy laden
Away we went along Collingwood Street
That's on the Road to Blaydon

Chorus:
Oh me lads, you should've seen us
  gannin'
Passing the folks along the road
  just as they were stannin'
Aal the lads and lasses there
  aal wi' smilin' faces
Gannin along the Scotswood Road
To see the Blaydon Races

Scotswood Road, 1962. Crowds turn out and traffic is brought to a standstill as the centenary anniversary of the Blaydon Races procession passes along Scotswood Road.

Scotswood, 1888. Servants enjoying refreshments after a shoot. Scotswood may have been viewed as a strictly working class area, but it still had a number of well-to-do families and one of the passions of the day was going on a shoot.

Scotswood, 1917. Workers from the Adamsez bathroom fitting factory in a jolly mood. They possess a military air and their soldier-style caps tell us the picture was probably taken during the First World War. Adamsez are reputed to have supplied bathroom fittings for the Kremlin in Moscow.

Above: Churchill Street, October 1900. Mutton at 5d per lb and best beef at 7d – that's what the tickets on display at the butcher's shop owned by the late Mr and Mrs James Hall Baird Gilroy, in Churchill Street, indicated. I'm afraid the modern Health and Safety Inspector would have had a field day with this meat display open to the elements, especially as there would have been no refrigeration for it to be stored overnight. But the shop workers themselves look to be clean and well attired for the job.

Opposite: West End, 1971. A typical street scene from the West End. These were the conditions that children played in.

Scotswood, 1936. A game of cricket would always draw a large crowd. The dog seems to be interested in the bowler's marker while the girls wait in the wings to see how their young men cope with the bat.

Scotswood, 1971. We have moved on twenty-five years but the only thing that's changed is the game. It is now predominantly football. The lads will be playing a game commonly known around Tyneside's back lanes as 'doors', which simply meant using the back doors as goals, one for each player.

Scotswood, 1971. Despite the dangers there is no more exciting place for a youngster to explore than a wrecked car. This youngster, closely attended by three dogs, is playing around a rubbish tip typical of the Scotswood area of that time.

Scotswood, c. 1952. Grim living conditions for residents of the 1950s. Children play in the dank, cobbled streets that seem to blot out any hint of sunshine. This area was marked for the great clearances to be replaced by a 'City in the sky' (high-rise flats) as part of the housing revolution of the 1960s promoted by T. Dan Smith (Mr Newcastle).

Scotswood, 1962. It may not be Lord's cricket ground, but these youngsters are just as determined to put on a great show of the hallowed game, albeit in a back lane in Scotswood, amid the washing lines and the interest of the neighbours.

Opposite above: Scotswood, April 1956. Neighbours chatting in a back lane beside walls that seem ready to crumble.

Opposite below: Pitt Street, 1950. As the slum clearance got under way, just off Barrack Road, small traders are given notice to quit their premises. Mr Matthew Hutchinson, umbrella-maker, hairdresser and one-time newsagent, said: 'I've been here for fifty years and it's not easy to start all over again when you are seventy-two.' Mr William Birchnall, who had run a paper shop and general store, after being blown up and incapacitated in a mining accident, said: 'What am I going to do now?' His question was echoed by Mr William Cowan, who had mended radios since 1931. 'I've never even had a notice to quit. What's going to happen to me?' A grocer for fifteen years, Mr John Giar asked the same question. More than three acres were levelled in the area bounded by Barrack Road, Derby Street and Stanhope Street.

Above: Scotswood, 1971. Life in the West End may have been grim, but these two ladies seem to be grinning and bearing it in Shumac Street, connected to the Richardson Leatherworks. Many residents had lived for more than fifty years in the homes that were due for demolition.

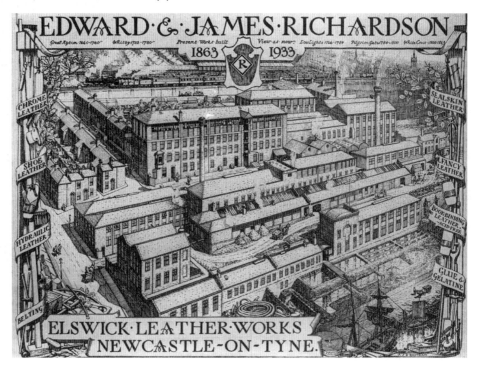

Above: Scotswood Road, 1900. This photograph shows Scotswood Road as a thriving thoroughfare. A horse and cart and handcart stay well away from the tram lanes, either side of the elegant power lines, which head into the city centre.

Above: Scotswood, *c.* 1940. The choir of St Margaret's church, Scotswood.

Opposite below: Scotswood, 1780. Richardson's leatherworks sited their first tannery just outside the city walls in 1780, but they soon moved inside the walls to the Scotswood Road/Elswick area, just on the banks of the Tyne which was vital for their supplies and transport.

Violet Street, overlooking Dunston power station, 1966. A plan to build an estate of houses on the steeply built sloping street had just been announced.

Scotswood, October, 1960. This picture was taken two years after Newcastle City Council declared war on its slums. If you look closely at the picture you can see two very small children at play around these dangerous half demolished buildings, indeed families were still living here and waiting to be re-housed while around them other homes were being pulled down.

The grim back-to-back housing of the Scotswood area of the early 1950s shown in all its reality. The smoke from the Dunston power station, across the River Tyne, blots out much of the light as well as creating an unhealthy environment for residents.

Gloucester Street, 1946. The street air-raid shelters just off Scotswood Road could be quickly accessed in a sudden air raid. After the war some of these shelters were used as street shops and storage units.

Armstrong Road, October 1960. The character of this road, running parallel to the River Tyne, changes three or four times during its mile and a half length. From tiny houses, converted into flats at one end, through a quiet part of the road that runs alongside Hodgkin Park, to the rows of council houses at the far end. Nobody would have called it the most beautiful street in the town, but most of the residents seemed to be contented in what could certainly be called a most unpretentious road. Mrs Elizabeth Featherstone, who had lived at No.77 for thirty-five years said: 'It really is very handy up here. You are not far away from the bank, handy for the shops.' But, as a direct contrast, at No.103, Mrs Martha Fleming said: 'I don't like living here, but you can't do anything about it unless you have plenty of money. Still I suppose you are lucky these days if you have a flat at all. Of course, we have no hot water and no baths, and there is an outside toilet.'

Central station, 1954. A gardener is at work on one of the new beds already mapped out.

Loadman Street, 1967. One of the wives of the street was quoted in the *Chroncile*, 'Once it was a lovely street. Nice people came here. Good, nice working–class churchgoers.'

Elswick Road, 1954. Full of character yet empty of life, that is apart from one shopper crossing the road and a few parked cars. Although a billboard in this picture says that 'Persil washes whiter than white', the buildings look decidedly grimy from the heavy industry which dominated the area.

Elswick, 1957. When families moved into the new blocks of flats behind Scotswood Road, Newcastle, the children found a new game – walking the boards. The boards are the floorboards in the derelict and semi-demolished old houses in Newcombe Street, behind the flats in Beaumont Street, Elswick and the game is to walk across them. If the boards are rotten, all the better, it makes it more exciting. The two rows of condemned houses are half demolished and children from the neighbourhood swarm over them. Luckily, apart from a few scrapes and bruises, nothing serious happened to these children, but it may have been a different story if a wall had collapsed or floorboards had given way. One young mother said that she spent half the day at the window watching her son play outside: 'I have told him time and time again to keep away from the houses, but it doesn't have any effect.' One of the girls standing on the steps said: 'The last time I was here I fell down the stairs and hurt my head. My mother doesn't know.'

Above: Elswick, *c.* 1900. Three children play in the gutter, while a fourth reclines in what appears to be a wheelbarrow. The only sign of traffic is two horses and a cart and loose scaffolding seems to be holding up the building in the background.

Top: Elswick Street East, 1959. Children risked being knocked over by cars using the street as a shortcut.

Overleaf: Elswick Street East, 1959. Parents stormed Newcastle town hall when the Slum Clearance Committee told fifty families with sixty to seventy children who'd been promised re-housing priority that this couldn't yet be implemented. The street had been condemned in 1936, but was eventually cleared in 1962.

The resurrection, by John Graham Lough, in Elswick Park, 1929.

Opposite above: Elswick Park, 1927. A Victorian relic seen beached here in Elswick Park. The barge had been retired after years of service, being used for surveys of the Tyne and for social jaunts. Gaily decorated with flags it carried many a merry company of men and women up and down the river Tyne.

Opposite below: The original caption to this photograph said 'giving Satan a spring clean', 1929. Another of John Graham Lough's statues, Lord Collingwood, stood near the mouth of the Tyne.

Elswick Lodge, *c.* 1970. These seem happy days for the Lodge, but from 1920 until 1969 it had been run by Newcastle Diocesan Council for Moral Welfare, as a mothers and babies home. It was alleged that many single mothers were separated from their babies who were then sent for adoption.

Opposite above: Elswick Road School, 1970. The old-fashioned Victorian façade of Elswick Road School, just by the junction with Bentinck Road.

Opposite below: The Elswick Park Institute, 1963. The institute houses the Elswick works library as well as the apprentices' welfare club. The sign in the middle of the building reads 'the Elswick Engine Works Mechanics Institute 1863'.

Elswick Hall, 1928. This massive Georgian mansion was originally built in 1810 for John Hodgson and was later the residence of Richard Grainger, then Christian Alihusen, the chemical manufacturer. He sold it to a group of men, including Sir William Haswell Stephenson and Joseph Cowen, who held it until the corporation took it over. Joseph Cowen was the founder of the *Newcastle Evening Chronicle*. The hall was originally the site of a priory. It was demolished in the late 1970s.

Elswick, 1938. A street entertainer who presented daily shows on the streets of Newcastle while trying to sell, or entice parents to buy, cheap toys for their children.

three

Cruddas Park
and Rye Hill

When T. Dan Smith came out with his bold City in the Sky plan for Newcastle, it brought a vision of futuristic styled housing, offices and shops on the Manhattan scale. But the grand plan collapsed because of corruption, bad design and inadequate building materials that ended with T. Dan Smith, also known as Mr Newcastle, being jailed. Only the Cruddas Park flats, on Scotswood Road, exist today in the West End as a legacy of this ill-fated 1960s building revolution that was to transform Newcastle into the 'Brasilia of the North.' At least Cruddas Park, named after George Cruddas, a director of the Armstrong armament factories at nearby Elswick, helped to sweep away some of the shambolic and unhygienic housing that existed in the area.

Noble Street flats, which stood in Rye Hill, were built in the 1950s and because of vandalism and the poor conditions the council proposed a new scheme in 1961 to upgrade the housing, landscape the surroundings, and create a safe haven for children to play in. But the high ideals once again proved groundless as seventeen years later the flats were demolished.

Rye Hill was a notoriously tough area where trouble waited around every corner. It had been the cheapest part of the city to live in and this shaped the area's abnormal social make-up. The area attracted the weak and poor. The suicide rate and the incidence of respiratory TB were three times the average for the rest of the city, while venereal disease was twelve times above the average. It was a gravitation point for many of Newcastle's problem families and five times as many lived in its average suburb. The area also contained a very high proportion of young families, with children under nine comprising about one in four of the total population. But it wasn't just the problem of clearing away the slums and rebuilding that faced the council because when the inhabitants were moved out to make way for demolition and rebuilding, it was obviously going to be hard to re-sell the area back to the former inhabitants, many of who had moved to the leafier suburbs of the city. Although there is still a long way to go, the area has been transformed by demolishing street upon street of back-to-back housing, giving fresh hope that, at last, things are moving in the right direction.

Cruddas Park flats, 1965. In the background can be seen the remnants of the back-to-back housing that was cleared away to facilitate the building of the Cruddas Park flats. The site has been landscaped with mature trees planted creating a vastly different environment from the dirty, smoke-ridden area that existed before.

Work is well underway on the Cruddas Park scheme in 1960. The site was previously occupied by St Vincent's Orphanage and was to create 144 dwellings.

Cruddas Park, 1962. Labour Party leader Hugh Gaitskell unveils a piece of sculpture at the Cruddas Park flats in 1962. It was created be Kenneth Ford of Leicester College of Arts after his design won a first prize of £250 in a nation-wide contest.

St Stephen's church, 1963. Not everything was cleared away by the bulldozer. The beautiful St Stephen's church, which stood in Clumber Street, now has only the steeple remaining but it is just as imposing and refuses to be dominated by the Cruddas Park flats.

Left: Rye Hill, 1966. The fate of St Mary's church was finally decided when the diocesan authorities and the trustees agreed to allow it to be demolished. Built in 1814 it was in an unsound condition and because of population shifts now left empty and at the mercy of vandals.

Below: Rye Hill, 1966. Housing that was soon to make way for the new developments planned for the area.

Opposite: Rye Hill, 1967. What dangers awaited these children playing in the decaying ruins?

Washday in a Noble Street back lane, 1955.

Above: Noble Street flats, 1977. By the time this picture was taken the flats had been practically sealed off from the city because of vandals cutting telephone lines. The flats suffered all the social evils of the time.

Opposite: Noble Street flats, 1973. You can't keep a good 'un down, as this picture shows. Three youngsters forget about the new playgrounds and make their own entertainment.

Left: Noble Street flats, 1970. The dream begins to turn into a nightmare as the forgotten flats are once again falling into disrepair.

Below left: Noble Street flats and a forlorn looking youngster stands alone in one of the stark long walkways, 1973.

Below right: Another young resident of the ill-fated Noble Street flats, 1973.

four

Park and Leisure

There was always plenty going on in the West End of the city. Besides the vast number of pubs, there was always the picture houses, works trips and, of course, the Empire theatre. But it was the pubs that this area of Newcastle was famous for.

Scotswood Road was known as the road of 100 pubs, but there were never more than forty-six at any one time. Also, because the road was nearly four miles long they used to say that even if a man had a pint in every pub it was impossible to get drunk - because the walk would sober him up. By the 1970s just about all the pubs had disappeared and by the 1980s the Armstrong's Elswicks works, which had indirectly brought them into being, had gone too. Within forty years of the arrival of the Armstrong business forty-seven city brewers had entered into a Scotswood Road bonanza, servicing twenty-eight hotels and eighteen beer houses.

The Road became as fiery as Armstrong's blast furnaces and its prosperity became dependent on the world's bloodbaths. If the Chinese, Croats and Serbs, or anyone else, went to war, the men of the West End of Newcastle made their armaments - and when they weren't working they were brawling! It is said that along the road there was a brawl on every corner, every Saturday night and Bank Holiday, sometimes they lasted for an hour. The police, it was said, were picked for their brawn, not brains: apparently P.C. Elija 'Ben' Goulden once made an arrest in Corporation Street but took the man to Pitt Street to charge him because he could not spell Corporation! The pubs were open from six in the morning until eleven at night. Furnace men were said to work up their thirst by drinking salt water. The moulders would meet in the Moulders Arms, the mechanics in the Mechanics. Stick lads ran all day between the works and the pubs with two dozen jugs of beer a time for the thirsty workers. One of the most notorious drinkers of Scotswood Road was, in fact, a woman - Mrs Tommy Turner. Even the big drinkers refused to try and out-drink her. Her husband Tommy, a convicted pig thief, made his living catching rats under the Scotswood Road jetty. He would then sell them to the Star Hotel rat pit to be the sport of the hounds in Westgate Road.

Barrack Road, c. 1900. These two fine gentleman with clean white aprons pose in the doorway of the Wellington Inn. The proprietor was George Blair and, according to the signs in the window, it was a Bass house.

A small crowd of children, most of them shoeless, gather outside The Crooked Billet in Scotswood Road, 1896. Maybe their dads were inside having a drink and they thought there was a chance of a copper or two – but it was more likely to be a slap around the ear. Of course, they could just as easily have been attracted by the camera.

Queuing for tickets at the Newcastle Empire in Westgate Road to see the American singing sensation, crooner Johnny Ray, 1955.

The Hydraulic Crane, one of the last pubs on Scotswood Road, *c.* 1958. This photograph shows the then manager, K. Flint and his wife Phemie (fourth from the left) with staff and customers. Molly Lake's family ran the pub from the turn of the century until 1958.

Sledging in Leazes Park, 1952. The greater the speed the bigger the thrill for David Collier, Douglas Chisholm and Gordon McNally. This was a park for all seasons as the next set of pictures shows.

A heavily laden boat speeds across the lake at Leazes Park in 1953, pursued by Peter the surfing swan. Apparently this swan rode the tidal wave produced by the boat every day.

A group of men play a game of dominoes one bright February day at Leazes Park in 1937.

Leazes Park, 1936. The boats are out and full of children but they are all under the watchful gaze of the eagle-eyed park keeper. Some are paddling, some are rowing and there is one lad, at the front right, who is fishing.

A couple take advantage of the Indian Summer with a stroll through Leazes Park in October 1951. This beautiful scene with the long shadows makes a perfect study in light and shade – only a few minutes walk away is the bustle of the city centre.

Left: A young girl called Lorna encounters a wooden man in Leazes Park, 1949.

Below: A works outing for the foremen of the Armstrong, Whitworth & Co. Ltd, *c.* 1900.

The King's Hall cinema in Marlborough Crescent, 1930. It is said to have been opened in 1905 by Joseph Collins and his two brothers and was thought to be the first permanent cinema in Newcastle. It had originally been the Drysdale Hall and in 1893 had become a Roman Catholic junior school. In 1908 the King's cinema was known as the 'cosiest hall in the city' when it re-opened after being redecorated at enormous expense. There were two performances each evening of 'superb pictures and high-class varieties', at seat prices of 2d. Bicycles were stored free for patrons. The press advertisements boasted no intervals or weary waits and no vulgarity or rowdyism at the King's. On the morning of 5 September 1930, the King's was destroyed by fire and because rebuilding had been in progress the owner had neglected to maintain the insurance.

Soldiers help clear the snow in Gallowgate, 1941. Massive snowstorms hit the North East, the worst since 1910. The first flurries occurred on 19 February when throughout Northumberland and Durham roads were blocked and traffic brought to a standstill. The January snow had just been cleared away when new storms started and, at one point, forty-five trams out of ninety-five on the Newcastle routes, were out of order.

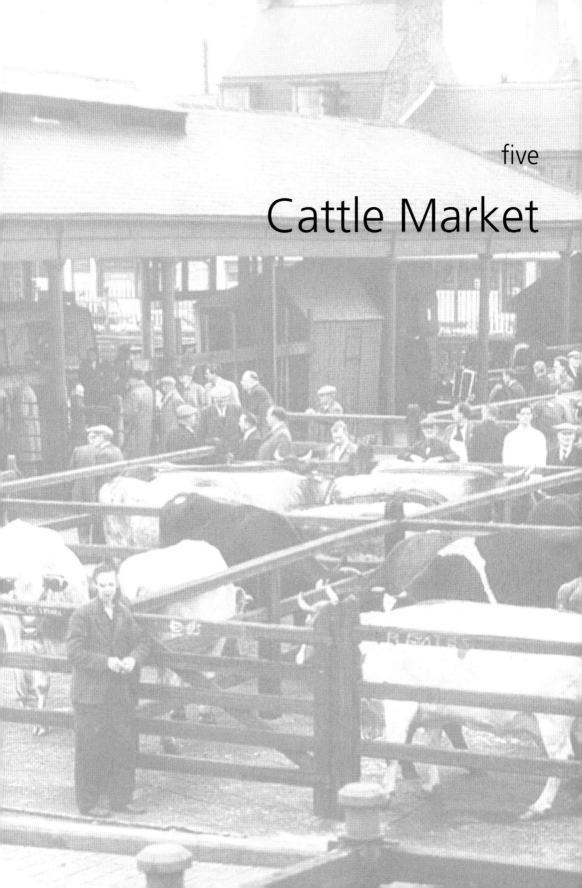

five

Cattle Market

Newcastle's cattle market has moved sites a few times although it has always remained in the same general area. The sheep and cattle markets were first held in 1830 around the Forth area of the city, west of central station. Before and, indeed, long after this time, the Newcastle butchers bought their cattle from Morpeth market, which was held every Wednesday but when Newcastle set up its own cattle market, Morpeth went out of business. In the 1920s when Marlborough bus station was built the market was moved to a new site on Scotswood Road. This was eventually closed and levelled for a car park in 1983. Now both Marlborough Crescent and the cattle market have disappeared under a regeneration plan.

The cattle market has a curious claim to fame as the scene of the first armed bank raid on Tyneside and one of the first in Britain. On Friday 2 June 1933, three armed Scotsmen tried to rob Lloyds Bank but it didn't turn out the way they had hoped. The robbers may have been armed but their ammunition was apparently too big for their guns. Their getaway plan consisted of three one-way tickets on an express train from the Central Station to Edinburgh! The robbers walked into the bank, locked the doors, produced their guns and demanded money. One of the clerks bombarded them with coins, injuring one of the hooded robbers. Another of the staff got out a message calling for the police but the message was received as a request for fire brigade assistance. One robber grabbed £300 out of a till and another descended into the strong room but became trapped when the door shut behind him. A third masked man burst into the manager's office but the staff overpowered him and the first robber and ending up sitting on them. The scene must have resembled a Keystone Cops film as the fire brigade arrived followed by a group of meat porters and abattoir labourers, armed with meat cleavers, all looking for a bit of the action. Then a police motorcycle patrolman arrived, with a sidecar companion, to conduct the arrests! Two of the robbers got ten years and the third a year. As a tailpiece, when bank officials came to tot up the missing loot they found that they were 7s 6d better off!

When this picture appeared in the *Newcastle Evening Chronicle* in 1929 it was captioned 'Room for more' - our photo of the cattle market bus stand taken this morning ... clearly shows that more use might be made of it.

Marlborough Crescent, 1955. Eventually there was a great deal more use made of the area as it became Marlborough Crescent bus station and the cattle market was moved to the south west of the site.

Marlborough Crescent, June 1947. Although on the same day crowds thronged central station, this station was deserted on what should have been one of the busiest travel days of the year in June 1947. The busmen were all on strike and the few people about found the place strangely quiet.

Marlborough Crescent, May 1948. The sun was out and day trippers were waiting for their bus to Blaydon, Crawcrook, High Spen and Hexham.

The caption accompanying this picture from the *Evening Chronicle* in 1953 said that although this could be a stockyard of the Argentine pampas or a Kansas prairie the picture was actually taken at the Newcastle Cattle Market.

Buyers checking and sellers hoping, at the cattle market in October 1960.

The cattle market re-opened for business in July 1964 after a break of fifteen years and business was brisk.

Newcastle meat market, January 1949. The weekend meat ration arrives to refill the hooks emptied over the Christmas period.

The new 'on the hook' system of marketing meat introduced by the corporation which replaced the old 'on the hoof' method, seen here at the meat market in 1955.

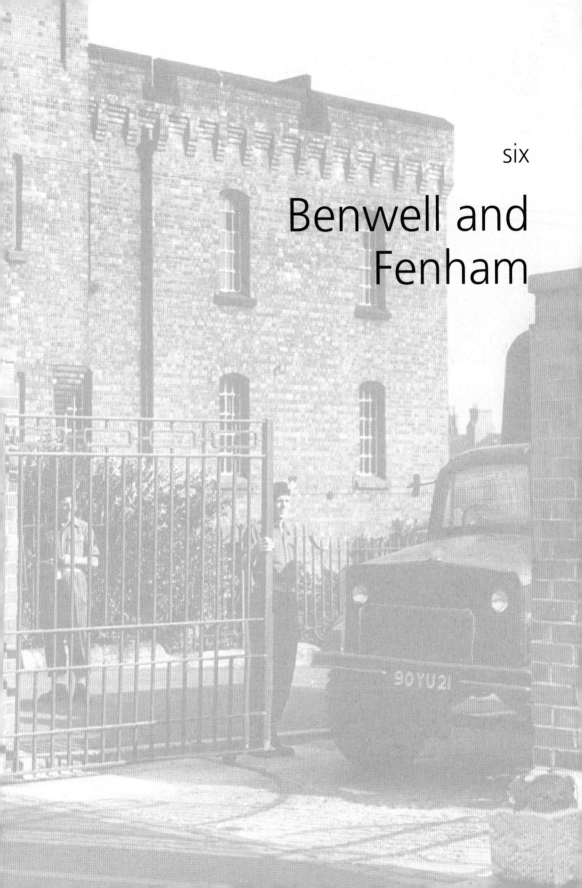

six

Benwell and
Fenham

Benwell and Fenham, along with the adjacent districts of Elswick and Arthurs Hill, form a western gateway into the heart of the City of Newcastle. Benwell has a history which goes as far back as the Roman occupation of Britain, is once again re-inventing itself. Its history has left strong legacies for an area which is now home for people of many different ethnic backgrounds. Just over a hundred years ago Benwell was one of the most important shipbuilding and engineering centres in the world. The movement away from heavy industry had threatened to devastate the area economically, but a new urban regeneration programme has replaced the former housing to give fresh hope to an area that is again developing a strong sense of community

Benwell first appeared in the record books just before the arrival of William the Conqueror. Then, when Henry VIII dissolved the monasteries the Crown took over ownership of Benwell from Tynemouth Priory in 1540, and in the early 1600s Benwell was split into smaller estates and eventually bought by the Shafto and Riddell families. This strengthened the connections with the Newcastle merchants who wanted to exploit the coal reserves on the banks of the Tyne. During the Civil War the invading Scottish army used the village of Benwell as a base for besieging Newcastle.

Fenham, one of the largest areas of the city, has a history that runs parallel to Benwell. The great hall, Fenham Hall, which gave its name to the area, was once owned by the Knights Templars. Upon the suppression of that Order in 1308 the will was granted by Parliament to the Hospitallers of St John of Jerusalem, but the burgesses of Newcastle claimed it in 1376 as parcel to the town held in farm of the Crown from time immemorial. They petitioned Parliament to that effect, asserting that in 1357 the Prior of Tynemouth had claimed Fenham as part of his manor of Elswick and been defeated. The affair was settled in 1404 in favour of the Hospitallers. In 1540, however, all their property was seized by Henry VIII and a few years later it was acquired by the Riddells, who sold it to the Ords. Fenham comes from the old English word for village on a flat area subject to lying water or flooding.

Contrasting styles of housing in Benwell, 1972.

Ready at last. This is the first public house named after the local hero Bobby Shafto, 1957. The people of Benwell had to wait over twenty years for Deuchars Ltd, then a subsidiary of Newcastle Breweries, to finish building this pub. Work started before the Second World War when foundations and cellars were completed, but the war held things up and then building restrictions followed in its aftermath.

Benwell Tower, 1947. This was once the home of the Shafto family, rebuilt in the nineteenth century by John Dobson and latterly the official residence of the Bishops of Newcastle, and most recently the Mitre Hotel. Today it is well known as the Byker Grove Youth Club, in the TV series *Byker Grove*, but in fact the building is at the other end of the city from Byker.

Top: Fenham Barracks, *c.* 1900.

Above: 'Eyes right' as fusilier recruits take the salute on parade at Fenham Barracks in December 1957.

Opposite above: Benwell Hall, seen here in 1978, was built in the late eighteenth century with extensions added later, probably by John Dobson. The original house was two storeys high and five bays wide and there were later additions on either side of the original block. William Surtees, brother of Bessie Surtees, occupied the house in the late eighteenth century. Only a few mature trees occupy the Hall's former site today.

Opposite below: Fenham Barracks, 1962. Associations with the army started way back in 1881 when the first fusilier recruits began pounding the square and learning to handle a rifle at Fenham. But in 1962 the barracks was heading for retirement as the fusiliers were given a new home in Sutton Coldfield. In 1958 the Fusilier Brigade was formed by grouping together the Royal Northumberland Fusiliers, the Royal Fusiliers and the Lancashire Fusiliers to make one new unit.

Fenham Barracks, 1961, and men of the Northumberland Fusiliers and the Royal Fusiliers line up for the Christmas dinner.

Above: St Robert's chapel looks spic and span as it is officially opened for worship at Fenham, 1930.

Opposite: 'Old Steamer' had been a great servant of Newcastle Corporation and it is seen here in its Benwell depot, in danger of being scrapped, in 1966. The engine had been lying idle in the Corporation yard for some time when the North of England Steam Traction Engine Society sought to restore it. This 15-ton Aveling Porter road roller was built in 1921 and took two hours to raise enough steam to work. It became a great favourite and was a regular prize-winner at local shows.

You can't keep a good 'un down. The 'Old Steamer' on official duty at Tyneside Festival, 1930.

An old view of Barrack Square, near Fenham Barracks, preserved from a lantern slide, *c.* 1900.

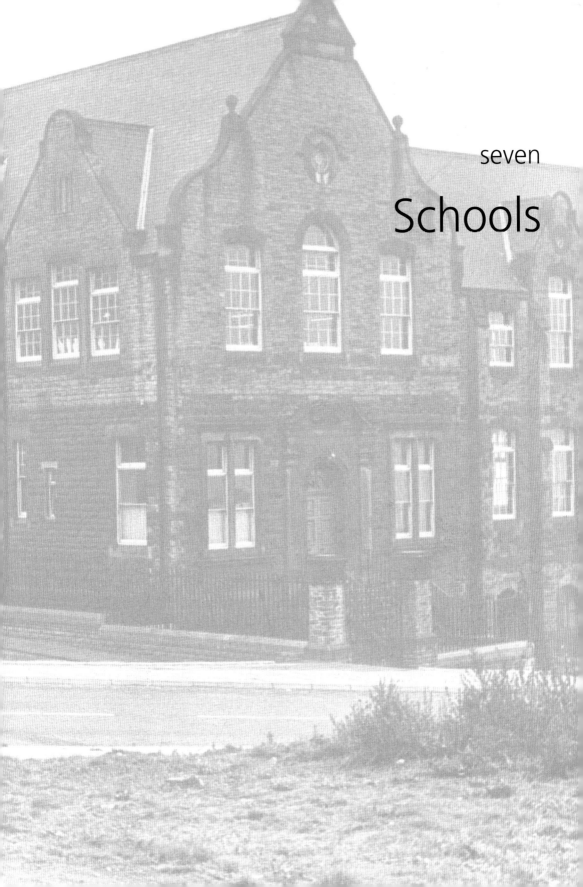

seven

Schools

In 1970 the *Newcastle Evening Chronicle* printed a story saying that the North had an acute primary school problem because of obsolete buildings and large classes. It also said that a third of primary school children were still being taught in nineteenth-century buildings. In January 1969, just over thirteen per cent of children were in bigger than regulation classes. i.e. nursery classes of more than twenty infants and junior classes of more than forty.

An expert in the field said that a child's sociological difficulties are often added to because of the old-fashioned school buildings they are taught in, such as the Atkinson Road school. The school, pictured in this chapter, while far from being run-down, was indisputably Victorian. The story called for a ten-year £100,000 cash programme to get the North's schools out of the doldrums.

Entrance to the Royal Free Grammar School, Spital, Newcastle.

Above: The Royal Grammar School of Newcastle seen in 1920. The school was situated in the old Hospital of St Mary the Virgin at the bottom of Westgate Road, where Neville Street now runs. Lessons in those days started at 6 a.m. and in winter pupils had to provide their own candles to work by.

Opposite above: A class of Westgate Hill Council School seen in 1918. In the picture are Sarah Gill, Vera Tempest, Doris May, Marjorie Devlin, Florence Sleight, Thomasina Osborne and Kenneth Ord. The headmaster of the school was known as 'Daddy' Shaw.

Opposite below: Rutherford High School for Girls, 1953. Pupils studying in cramped conditions, concentrate on their textbooks during lessons in the school library.

A wing of Rutherford College under construction, Bath Lane, *c.* 1910.

Above: The commemorative stone laying of a new technical wing for Rutherford College by the Antarctic hero, Sir Ernest Shackleton, 23 November 1909. Looking on is Alderman Johnstone Wallace, chairman of the college committee.

Left: Men work on the road beside Rutherford College, Bath Lane, 1929.

Above: South Benwell School in 1970. This imposing structure overlooks an area where all the old housing has been swept away.

Left: Canning Street School, just off Condercum Road and seen here in 1970, was built in 1904.

Left: Atkinson Road School, 1970. This Victorian school was affectionately known to its pupils as Akky Road School.

Below: Cambridge Street School, just off Scotswood Road, was hit by an outbreak of food poisoning in 1960. Altogether 150 children and teachers were affected by the outbreak. Seventy-six children were kept in hospital, although none were seriously ill.

Pupils perform folk dances on the school field at Dame Allan's, 1924.

Opposite above: A class in the lecture hall, which later formed part of the library, at Dame Allan school for girls, 1910.

Opposite below: One of the earliest group pictures to be taken at Dame Allan's school, 1909.

Pupils study in the library at Dame Allan's boys school, 1960.

The main entrance of Dame Allan's School, 1960

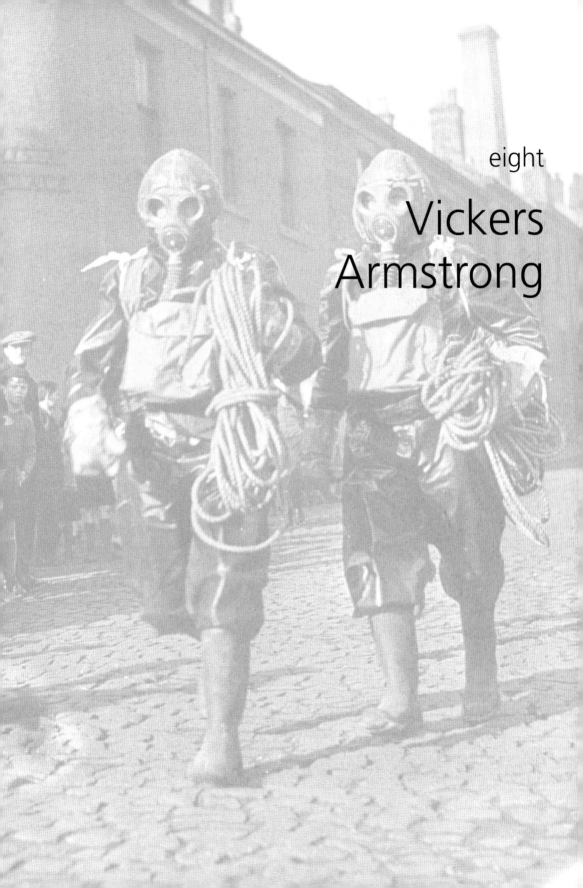

eight

Vickers
Armstrong

Lord Armstrong's Elswick works was founded in 1847. William George Armstrong had been making advances with hydraulics and, with an order from Newcastle Council, had converted a quayside crane to hydraulic operation. The success of this project enabled the start of a hydraulic machinery production at Elswick Works. During the Crimean War, Armstrong developed a revolutionary design for a rifled breech loading, built-up gun, which proved so successful and accurate that the Government ordered them for production at the works.

Andrew Noble joined Lord Armstrong in the business in 1860. Noble later became Sir Andrew Noble, for his development of artillery propellants. The company gained contracts for arming ships that were being built by Charles Mitchell & Co. In 1883 they took over Charles Mitchell & Co. to form Sir W.G. Armstrong Mitchell & Co. Ltd and opened a shipyard at Elswick which was closed after the First World War. In 1898 the firm was amalgamated with Sir Joseph Whitworth & Co., becoming Sir W.G. Armstrong, Whitworth & Co. Ltd. The order books were filled during first the South African War (1899-1902) and then the First World War. In 1898 the firm was then amalgamated with Vickers Ltd, becoming Vickers–Armstrong's Ltd. More products were developed between the wars, including coal-handling equipment, dock and water works equipment, hydraulic high pressure pumping plant, cranes and coal-handling equipment. The Second World War saw the firm exclusively assisting with the war effort. Since 1945 there has been a wide diversity of products and engineering facilities produced by the firm. The works was finally demolished in 1980. The King's Meadows was later dredged away to make way for the building of larger ships at the Elswick yards, including battleships.

A panoramic view of Elswick's shipyard in 1887. The ship being constructed is HMS *Victoria*.

Opposite above: Elswick works, *c.* 1860.

Opposite below: Elswick shipyard before the Second World War. The works were demolished in 1980.

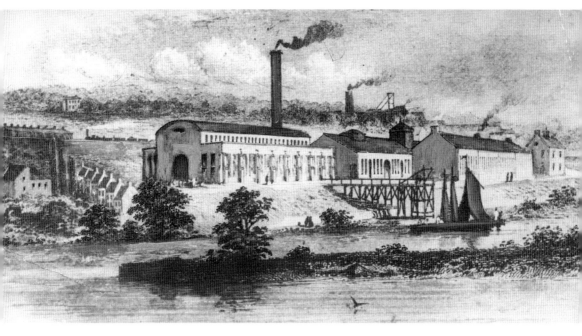

In the early 1900s one of the Royal Navy's proudest moments was the Spithead Review, a time for pomp and ceremony for the fleet in all its finery. But the Tyne-built HMS *Superb* nearly missed the 1909 review. The construction of the 22,300-ton Bellerophon Class battleship, laid down in February 1907, was delayed by a labour dispute at the Armstrong Whitworth Elswick yard. She was handed over in June 1909, just in time for the review on 31 July.

Opposite above: All the 'big guns' visited the Elswick works in 1877. The US Civil War hero and former President General Uylsses S. Grant, is seen here, fifth from left, on a visit to Newcastle in the late 1800s. The General is with Tyneside arms magnate, Sir William Armstrong (far right) and other guests, including Lady Armstrong stand in front of a giant artillery piece at Sir William's Scotswood works.

Opposite below: Crowds gather as the newly built HMS *Victoria* heads down the Tyne through an open Swing Bridge in 1890. There are no guns fitted to the turrets at this stage so the ship may be going for its first sea trials before returning to have them fitted.

Left: This photograph, taken from a glass negative, shows the battle cruiser *Invincible* leaving the mouth of the Tyne after being built by Armstrong Whitworth at Elswick in 1907. The 17,250-ton ship took part in the First World War battle of the Falklands and was eventually sunk at Jutland in May 1916.

Below: Vickers Armstrong's Ltd, *c.* 1941. Massive gun turrets for battleships come together at the Elswick works during the Second World War.

HMS *Eagle* was converted from a partially-built Chilean battleship *Almirante Cochrane* at the Elswick shipyard, *c.* 1917. She had been laid down at Elswick on 20 February 1913, but all work ceased in 1914 and she lay on her slip until 1917 when the Admiralty negotiated a purchase from the Chilean government for £1,334,358. Her design was modified to an aircraft carrier. She was launched on 8 June 1918 and commissioned on 26 February 1924. HMS *Eagle* was sunk on 11 August 1942 after being hit by four torpedoes from the German submarine U73 while escorting a convoy to Malta. Her engine room instrument dials were displayed only in Spanish and in metric measurements.

Chinese sailors attend the launch of the *Ching Yuan* at the Elswick shipyard, 1886. Over 600 officers and crew of the Imperial Chinese Navy sailed to Tyneside in 1887 to collect two cruisers. A number of those sailors were hit by what was known locally as 'a malady peculiar to the Chinese'. Two of the sailors, Lien Chin Yuen and Ching Shou Fu, died in Newcastle Infirmary and were buried at dawn by forty shipmates who carried their coffins from the hospital near Marlborough Crescent to St John's Cemetery at Elswick. A third died some days later.

Vickers Armstrong's Ltd, December 1942. The twin 15-inch gun turret of HMS *Abercrombie* nearing completion at the Elswick works. HMS *Abercrombie* was the last of forty-two Monitors to be built by the Royal Navy. Monitors were described as a poor man's battleship. They had a shallow draft and heavy armour and were built for land bombardment and unsuitable for use on open seas. HMS *Abercrombie* was designed to correct some faults of the previous monitors. Her upgraded 15-inch guns, increased deck armour, more AA guns and better arcs of fire for the 4-inch twin mounts and a taller funnel. She was launched on 31 March 1942 and, after turbine problems, completed on 5 May 1943. *Abercrombie* immediately steamed to the Mediterranean to give support to the allied landings in Sicily.

Above and below: Gun turrets being assembled for battleships at the Elswick works, 1938.

A 100-ton gun being lowered into the SS *Europa* on 18 July 1876, under the Elswick sheerlegs (floating crane) for transportation to Spezia, Italy. The *Europa* was the first ship to pass through the newly opened swing bridge at Newcastle which was also built at Elswick works.

An early muzzle-loading gun made at the Elswick works, *c.* 1870. The gentleman in the picture is Mr Henry Hutchinson, who was in charge of the gun finishing department. There are also three different types of shell on display.

A 12-inch, rail-mounted howitzer is made ready for the front during the First World War at Elswick works, *c.* 1915.

14-inch gun barrels in production at the Elswick plant, 1938.

A glorious sight for the British Army in the Second World War, a Scotswood factory full of 25-pounder field guns, 1942. It was the mainstay of the campaign that was laid down at the Battle of El Alamein. In February 1940 this factory's output for the gun was three per month; by 1942 it had risen to 100 per month.

Above: Gun barrels being turned out for the army and navy in 1942.

Left: Vickers Armstrong's factory, 1942. Vickers was responsible for the inception and design of the Valentine Tank. By stepping up production at the Elswick works the supply of tanks expanded to a monthly output of thirty-one by 1942. When the tank first went into production its armament consisted of one two-pounder gun and one 7.92mm BESA machine-gun. Eventually it was fitted with one 75mm gun as well as the machine-gun. Probably the greatest compliment which was paid to the men of Tyneside who designed the tank was when Russia, in the hour of its greatest need, sent a cable to the British Government, saying: 'Send us more Valentines'.

This page and opposite: There's plenty of patriotic spirit on display among these ladies turning out munitions at the Scotswood plant during the Second World War. Thousands of women helped keep the factory working twenty-four hours a day, turning out the hardware for Britain's armies fighting overseas. During the six years of war the factory turned out 620 Naval gun mountings, 15,899 guns, 3,224 gun carriages, 2,657 tanks, 11,726,000 fuses, 7,406,000 cartridge cases, 794,723 empty shells, 30,810 bombs, 33,728 HP air bottles, 22,456 hydraulic pumps and engines and 18,731 aircraft undercarriages.

Above: A 5-ton bomb made at Elswick works in July 1946.

Below: As well as the millions of artillery shells, bombs and fuses that were turned out during the Second World War, Vickers Armstrong's also had an important part to play in the production of Barnes Wallis's highly secret and successful bouncing bomb of the 'Dambusters' raid. Parts of the bouncing bomb were made at Sheffield, but it all came together at Scotswood. It was so secret that even those assembling the bomb did not know until after the raid what it was all about.

Above: The children of Scotswood have a worried look on their faces here in 1939 as they watch an ARP exercise in the Scotswood Road area. War is only a few months away and is this a taste of things to come?

Below: As Europe sinks into chaos and Britain prepares for war with Nazi Germany, work pushes ahead with the building of air raid shelters at the Scotswood works in 1939.

The company was very prominent in the production of steam locomotives. Their steam engines were used all over the world including India and South America, as well as extensively throughout Britain. Two locomotives built at Scotswood are seen here being loaded onto a river barge on the Tyne, c. 1929.

Above: One of the main machine shops at Armstrong, Whitworth & Co. turns out locomotive parts in large quantities, 1936.

Opposite: A giant of Scotswood Road – this powerful crane is viewed by prominent industrialists as it lifts a ship's gun turret, weighing 102 tons, into place, 1915.

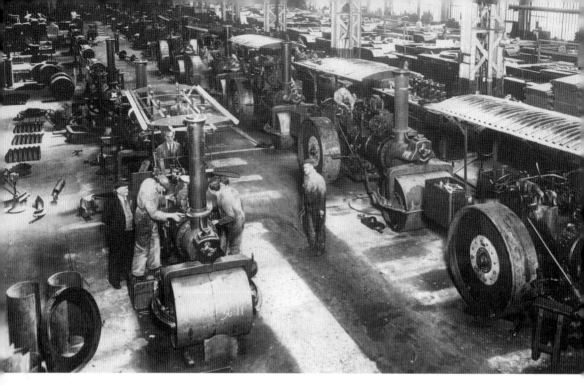

Steamroller production at the Scotswood plant was soon rivalling arms production in 1946 as the peace dividend began to come into fruition with the ending of the Second World War.

Tractor production at Vickers Scotswood plant was arousing business interest here in 1959. The company's experience in building tanks came in useful for the production of the caterpillar tracked farm vehicles.

Above: Machines which had only months previously been stamping out cartridges for war were, as peace broke out, stamping out aluminium pans for the home, 1946.

Right: Huge man cages, each consisting of four decks and made of duralumin, were constructed at the Elswick works. They were built in 1936 for the Daggafontein mines of South Africa. Each cage was 26ft 11in. high, weighed 3.5 tons and were capable of carrying eighty men.

Left: A van standing in the foreground is dwarfed by a giant hydraulic coal hoist built at the Elswick works, *c.* 1925. There were similar ones being made at the time for the Great Western Railway and Leith Docks Commission.

Below: All in their overalls, women workers at the Armstrong Whitworth factory in Elswick, *c.* 1900.

Women of the Armstrong factory school pictured with their tutors, 1918.

A women's soccer team formed by workers of 43 shop, Armstrong's factory on Scotswood Road, 1918. They were probably munitions workers and it is thought that on one occasion they played at St James' Park.

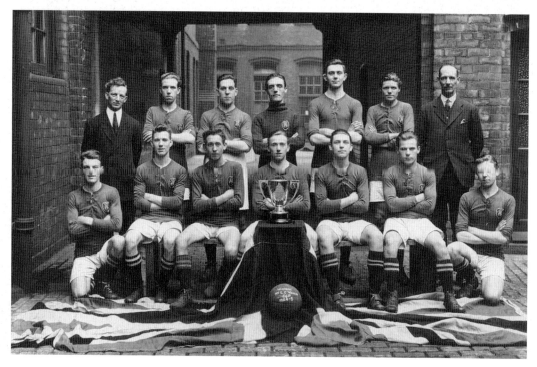

The Vickers Armstrong's team that won the 1924/25 North East Coast Welfare Cup.

Vickers Armstrong's won the Tyneside Works Welfare League in 1925/26.

One of Vickers Armstrong's teams in training, *c*. 1936.

The Vickers Armstrong's gym team, some wearing their medals, before a training session, *c*. 1920.

The Vickers Armstrong's gym team pose for the camera, *c.* 1920.

A tough session at the Elswick Works Apprentice Club, 1919.

T. Fagan puts on a somersault display at the Congers sports day, 1930.

Above: Vickers workers relax with games of billiards and snooker, *c.* 1920.

Overleaf: Billiards in progress at the Elswick Works apprentice club, *c.* 1919.

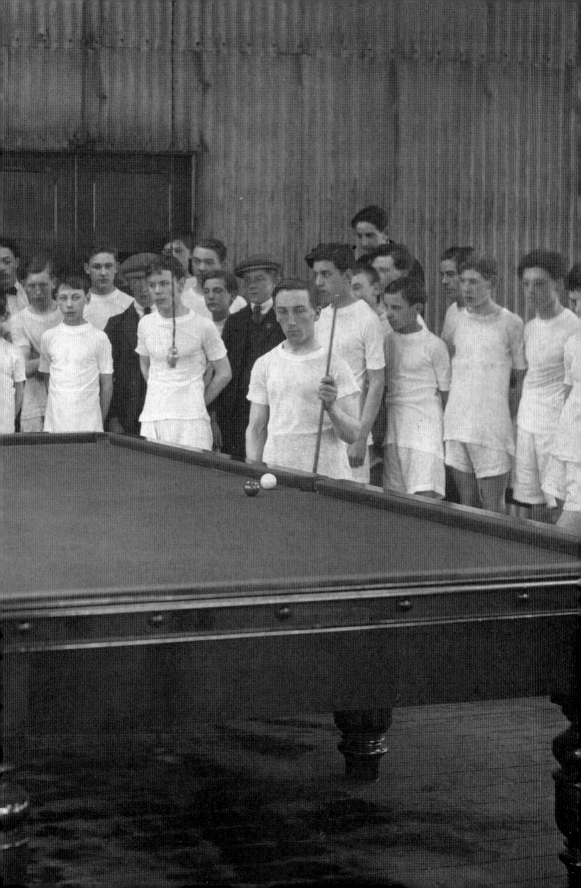

Lads from the Elswick Works apprentice club rowing on the Tyne, 1919.

nine

Of a Royal
Occasion

The royal family always got a real Geordie welcome when they visited the North East. We always assume that they are not allowed to see anything controversial and anything that may offend is removed from royal view. But you just have to look at the Prince of Wales, later to become the Duke of Windsor, as he visits Rye Hill, one of the poorest areas of Tyneside, to see that this was not always so.

The popular Prince of Wales may have abdicated the throne and rejected his chance of becoming King, but the public always thought he cared about their plight. When unemployment was at its peak he insisted on touring the poor areas of Tyneside, as well as pit villages, to show his support for those who expected to become his subjects. But because of his association with Wallace Simpson, an American divorcee, he turned his back on the throne and his place was taken by his brother, who became King George VI.

But this did not hinder any of the traditions of close loyalties with the North, as the Queen had strong ties with the area. The King came to the throne shy and unused to public speaking but with the guidance of the Queen he overcame this to become a loved and respected war-time leader.

Above: King George VI and Queen Elizabeth visited the General Hospital on Newcastle's Westgate Road in 1939 and were given a guard of honour by the nurses.

Opposite above: The Queen was the centre of attention as the nurses studied her every move as the royal couple left the hospital.

Opposite below: A gale is blowing as Queen Elizabeth inspects Civil Defence workers at St James' Park during the Second World War. She elegantly makes sure the royal hat stays in place although her attendant seems to be having a bit more difficulty, *c.* 1941.

During a visit to Tyneside, the Prince of Wales, later the Duke of Windsor, shows his support for the unemployed as he chats to residents at Rye Hill, 1932.

The Prince of Wales runs the gauntlet of residents who turned out in force to see the royal visitors at Rye Hill in 1932.

Above and below: It was all hands on deck as residents of Pine Street set to work decorating their streets ready for Coronation day in 1953. There were women brooming the cobbled streets and pavements, standing on chairs and men up ladders putting everything in place. Children watched, amazed as the bunting went up and royal emblems and union flags went into place.

This picture was described in the newspaper on 7 May 1935 as 'a gay scene at an open-air party in Centre Street, Gallowgate'. Everyone was celebrating the twenty-fifth anniversary of the accession to the throne of King George V.

There was plenty to celebrate with the ending of the First World War in 1918. The ending of four years of tragic losses in France was good enough reason for the nation to let its hair down. It was a time for potted plants, tea urns, best cups and plateful after plateful of cakes. Tyneside Terrace, in Elswick, was part of a little corner of Newcastle with a lead works, an Anglo-American petrol pump, a gas yard and a shipyard.

ten

Bits and Pieces

This chapter is a miscellany of photographs from the West End of Newcastle that don't fit logically into other chapters so here they are altogether: The colliers heading up the Tyne to take on their cargo, the scullers giving a glimpse of the sport that once commanded crowds of over 100,000 for Tyne races. There is also a picture showing the majestic poses of sprinters that may look as if they are just putting on the style for the camera, but with the large amounts of money wagered on a race, they were deadly serious in their endeavours.

A collier, probably on its way up to Dunston Staithes, passes Elswick lead works in 1957. The lead works, originally set up by Richard Fishwick of Hull, was situated in the Forth Banks area of Newcastle. Walkers, Parker & Co. had the largest lead works in England. History paints a vivid picture of the early times, such as the difficulties over land ownership which bedevilled a funeral corpse and cortege trying to pass over land owned by someone else and having to pay a penny toll to get the procession to the cemetery.

Opposite below: This strange contraption, seen here in Throckley in around 1900, was known as a dandy cart and was an integral part of the one horse-powered railway, linking the brickworks with the riverside quay. This was from Throckley brickworks and the trucks would be loaded with bricks and would run down an incline to the riverside, taking with them horse-riding on the dandy cart. The trucks would be emptied, the horse then got down from the cart, which had a low chassis, and pulled them up the slope.

Above: Coxed fours shooting the Scotswood Bridge at the end of a heat in the Joseph Cowen Cup at the Tyne Regatta, *c.* 1913. The *Newcastle Chronicle* Challenge Cup had been won outright by J. Higgins in 1911 and in its place, Joseph Cowen, proprietor of the *Newcastle Evening Chronicle*, presented the Joseph Cowen Challenge Cup to the Tyne Amateur Rowing Club to be competed for in the Tyne Regatta.

Above: Four sprinters lining up at the Victoria Running Ground near the Newcastle end of the old Redheugh Bridge on Good Friday 1894. This is the start of one of the heats and pictured, left to right, are J, Bright (Newcastle), J. Redshaw (Durham), Robert Gordon and J.G. Hutchinson (Newcastle). Robert Gordon, aged eighteen years, won the £100 foot handicap.

Above: King Edward Bridge carries the County Boundary sign between County Durham and Northumberland leading into the West End of Newcastle. This photograph is from 1958.

Below: The Japanese battleship *Hatsuse* which was launched at Armstrong, Whitworth & Co. in Elswick, passes through an open swing bridge on her way to sea trials in 1901. The stack was lowered to clear the High Level Bridge. Designed by Phillip Watts she was laid down on 10 January 1898. Before sailing to Japan the battleship represented the Emperor at Queen Victoria's funeral. She sank with the loss of 496 men on 15 May 1904 off Port Arthur, damaged by Russian mines.

Opposite below: Because of the complexity of the site and the restricted access at the two main entrances, Lord Armstrong's Elswick Works maintained its own fire brigade until 1982. These two firemen were photographed in around 1900.

Other local titles published by Tempus

Jarrow
PAUL PERRY

Jarrow was once a sparsely populated area which swelled to a population of 40,000 when industry boomed in the 1920s. Around ten years later, Jarrow faced decline. Using a fascinating collection of over 200 images, this book shows the rise, unexpected fall and further rise of Jarrow. Professional photographer Paul Perry also compiled *Jarrow Then & Now*, a pictorial history charting the changing face of the town and its skyline.
0 7524 3336 9

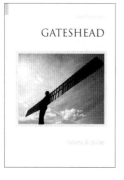

Gateshead History & Guide
ALAN BRAZENDALE

This book describes Gateshead's history from Roman settlements, through its industrial days when Dr Johnson unflatteringly described it as 'a dirty lane leading to Newcastle' to the modern Gateshead, famous for its International Stadium, Angel of the North, and Baltic Centre for Contemporary Art. This is an honest portrayal written from the heart of one of Gateshead's loyal citizens, who is not only a local historian but also a former Mayor of Gateshead.
0 7524 3207 9

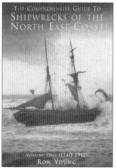

Shipwrecks of the North East Coast, Volume One (1740-1917)
RON YOUNG

Sailors have always known the danger that both life at sea and the odd voyage into deep waters can bring. In this book, Ron Young, an experienced diver of many years, catalogues the demise of many ships along the north-east coast of England, from Whitby to Berwick-upon-Tweed, and tells the story of their last journey. He assesses the potential of the wrecks as dive-sites and remembers the bravery of lifeboat crews in this comprehensive and engrossing book.
0 7524 1749 5

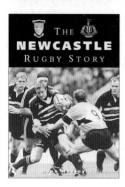

The Newcastle Rugby Story
ALAN HEDLEY

Rugby in the North East has a long illustrious history and intertwined with it is the story of the Newcastle club now known universally as The Falcons. This book remembers some of the club's key moments, and passionate players. Written by Alan Hedley, a rugby journalist based in Newcastle for the last twenty-five years, this book is an essential read for any sport or rugby fan in the North East.
0 7524 2046 1

If you are interested in purchasing other books published by Tempus, or in case you have difficulty finding any Tempus books in your local bookshop, you can also place orders directly through our website
www.tempus-publishing.com